The First-born

The First-born

AND OTHER POEMS

by Jack Davis

ANGUS AND ROBERTSON

First published in 1970 by
ANGUS AND ROBERTSON (PUBLISHERS) PTY LTD
221 George Street, Sydney
54 Bartholomew Close, London
107 Elizabeth Street, Melbourne
167 Queen Street, Brisbane
89 Anson Road, Singapore
Reprinted 1971

Published with the assistance of the Commonwealth Literary Fund
National Library of Australia
card number and ISBN 0 207 12088 9

Registered in Australia for transmission by post as a book
PRINTED IN AUSTRALIA BY HALSTEAD PRESS, SYDNEY

Introducing the Author

[From the transcript of a tape-recording made by Jack Davis in an interview with Richard Beilby]

MY FATHER, whose name was William Davis, was taken out of a tribe and reared up by a white family until he was the age of fifteen, then he left this family and worked all over the North-west and eventually came south. He was a remarkably good athlete and it was athletics which kept him within the white community, really.

My mum was taken away from her tribe in Broome by a white family, and reared up by them until she was fourteen or fifteen years of age, when she came to work in the south of the State for a white family. There she met my father and they got to know one another and became married. They lived in Northam for the first few years and then they came to Perth and this is where I was born.

We stayed in Perth until I was about eleven or twelve months of age and they went down to the south-west of this State where they stayed until my father died. It was in the south of the State that I had my schooling. My dad, as I said, was a good athlete: he played football for a country town and he was a prominent footballer. I went to school in a little mill town called Yarloop. I had the average Australian education, white Australian education; had eight years of school, but four months after I left school, my father was killed in an accident with a bull in which his neck was broken and he died instantly. This left the family with no bread-winner; and the boys—I had four brothers beside myself—we scattered all around the State. It was in the 'thirties, when there was a depression on and times were particularly hard, especially if you were part-aboriginal, but we managed to keep ourselves in work. Then Mother and the remainder of the family—the girls, five girls—shifted to the wheat-belt to a place called Brookton and there they stayed until my mum died. Of course, by then all the girls had grown up and got themselves married, and so had most of my brothers.

I went back into the timber district and worked there for a number of years, but really didn't find much satisfaction in it. I gained a Second-class Engine Driver's Certificate while I was working in one particular mill at a place called Boddington and then I decided to go north, which I did do, and I was ten and a half years in the North-west. I had a go at everything, just about everything that anybody does up there. I was windmill-man, breaking horses, boundary riding, went droving, was a drovers' boss for a while, was head-stockman on a couple of stations. The pay wasn't much but I loved the life because it was in the open and I worked amongst full-blood people for the first time and I think that this was when I really became interested in writing as a means of expression. Of course, most of those stations have good libraries and we always had access to the libraries, and as I was always treated as one of the white stockmen I ate and slept with them and not in the camps on the rivers or on a bare piece of red earth.

I always felt sorry for the full-blood aboriginal people because I often wondered how they did exist. They weren't paid any wages: they were given boots, a pair of trousers and a shirt and their tucker was mainly dry bread and boiled mutton. This was the usual fare on most stations for these people; in fact on some of the stations where I have worked I asked them why didn't they ask for better conditions, and when they did, I got myself into trouble with my employers. I was told quite often that if I didn't shut my mouth I would be black-balled in this particular district.

Being young and being rather timid in nature when you're only eighteen years of age, I had to be very careful. But the whole thing did make me see that there was something wrong with the set-up, in the pastoral areas at least, for our aboriginal people. They weren't paid wages, they were treated more or less as black slaves. I think these things did creep into my early writings, the injustice of it. Even in the towns, they had to leave town at six o'clock, which is at least an hour before sundown; they had to be off the streets. If they weren't, they were jailed by special laws which affected aboriginal people only and this caused considerable resentment. On one occasion I decided to see what I could do about fighting this so I got twelve other aboriginal boys with me and we stood on one street in a particular North-west town and I told them that we wouldn't move when the police arrived. Eventually, two police came along and said, "Boys, you've got to get off the street at six o'clock." I said, "We're not going. We've as much right here as anybody else." He warned me again and I refused so he warned me again and I looked around for my friends and they'd all fled, all walked off and left me to myself. Of course, I was jailed for the offence as being the ringleader and was given four days imprisonment. I refused to pay the fine, so I did the four days: the only satisfaction that I did get was that I didn't give the Government the money for my fine, in fact they had to feed me while I was there.

After leaving the North-west, I came south again and I started to write a lot more seriously than I had done in the past and I saved lots of pieces of verse. With the aftermath of the war, like the rest of the world, even aboriginal people were looking for something better and the Government made a genuine attempt to do something for the twenty-five or twenty-six thousand aborigines in Western Australia. They went about it the wrong way and I could see that they were going about it the wrong way so I decided to get somehow wrapped up in aboriginal affairs. This was all a new field to me because there were so many things which needed to be done, so much Government apathy had to be hacked at and also the apathy of the white Australian public had to be attacked. We're still attacking it now.

This is the reason why I decided to do something about aboriginal affairs and the first real chance I got was when I got the chance of working for the Aboriginal Advancement

Council and got the support of a few but a very dedicated band of people to help in this matter. They are helping now, by throwing continually up to the Government, and the public, the malfunctions which do creep in, and drawing attention to the practices which government departments adopt in dealing with aboriginal people which do not help to advance them at all, in fact hold them down. I feel that this has brought out a lot of bitterness in me. I think I can control this bitterness; I know that a lot of our aboriginal people can't, which they can't be blamed for. Most people say it's a "chip on the shoulder", but I think there are other phrases you can use because this is rather hackneyed and tends to imply that you are wrong to have a chip on your shoulder. I think that the reason why we have this bitterness towards white society is because as long as white settlement has been in W.A., which is what I am concerned about mainly, because I live here, the maltreatment and the mistakes have been going on; and they are still going on. We are one of the most affluent countries in the world and we have one of the highest living standards, yet we have the highest mortality rate in the world in regards to our indigenous people. This shows that there is something radically wrong with white administration in Australia in regard to the aboriginal population which, I know, only represents two and a half per cent of the over-all population itself. This is what is really the cause of aboriginal troubles at present and I firmly believe that people who can write, whether they are white or coloured, no matter what type of Australian they are, should do so about these matters. If we can make a concentrated attack upon Government apathy towards infant mortality amongst aboriginal people, housing for aboriginal people and education, we can uplift the aboriginal people to the standard of their white counterparts.

But to get back to my childhood at Yarloop, what I really liked about that time was that we were a family that had a lot of freedom. Not the freedom that whites had, but we had good parents, there was always plenty of food, wholesome food at least. Now and again there were lean days, but my dad was a man who worked in the same job for sixteen years. On weekends, we would—me and my brothers—away we would go in the bush and we would walk for miles and miles and we would have a wonderful time. Sometimes some of our neighbours' boys would come with us and we would do all the things that country boys do. Looking back on it, I can see that my imagination was much more vivid than theirs and I think I used to live in a really fantastic world of my own. I mean, to find a bird's nest and to know there were eggs in it— their ambition would be to climb the tree and take the eggs or throw stones, but mine wasn't: I used to always go back and wait for the young ones to hatch. Things like this.

This was clover country, wonderfully green. The clover used to grow so high that it would almost trip you on your face, and I used to pull up the clover to look for things under- neath such as long-stemmed mushrooms. I had ideas that there were things, well, another world living in the roots of the grass and things like that. If I saw a plant coming out of the ground—I might just see the head of the plant—and I'd scrape away a bit of the ground and come back next day to see how far it had grown out of the earth. Not far from where we lived, there was a huge swamp and on it there were hundreds of dabchicks; quite a few ducks also landed there, but the dabchicks were the ones that nested there. I used to test the mother dabchicks by swimming out and getting about eight eggs from other nests and putting them all in one nest, and the poor old mother dabchick used to have to try and clutter up and cover these eggs; and since she's only a small bird—well, I can never recall the eggs not having been hatched out because no sooner was the dabchick born than they were gone, slip into the water and swim away immedi- ately. These were the sort of things I used to get up to.

At school I used to get on well with my teachers, but even at the age of ten, when most kids used to go to bed with comic books or books like *Huckleberry Finn*, I used to go to bed with a dictionary because I loved words and wanted to under- stand words. Yarloop was a small town and at the school there were at least four classes in one room; you know, fourth standard up to the eighth class. The headmaster would be teaching the eighth class in English, for instance, and he would ask them to spell a word like "cosmopolitan". If they wouldn't then he'd yell out to me and say, "We'll ask Jack out of the Fourth Standard if he can spell it." I'd jump up and spell the word "cosmopolitan". Of course, they used to chase me round the school-ground for this, in fact some of them used to bribe me with lollies and oranges, if I was asked to next time, to muff it so that they wouldn't look so stupid. I did well in most grades, but education in those days was just to get you through till you were fourteen and then you left school and looked for work, whether you were white or coloured.

Going home from school we had to walk about four miles and it was a bush track. I knew every stump, every tree and I think I knew every stone and every bird along it. Poems about incidents such as "The Boy and the Robin", which really happened, come from that time. It was my love of Nature, even my experiments with different growths—I remember becoming awfully sick because I found a new tea which grew in the bush. I boiled it up in a jam-tin, mixed the tea, drank it and was very sick because this bush made a sweet liquid. I had named this "nigger-tea", drank it as an experiment and became awfully sick and also got a belt over the ear off Mum when I got home.

Along with being rather a fanciful child, I had, I think, suffered from quite a few periods of illness when I was a youngster, more than other members of the family. I was inclined to have horrible dreams, nightmares, and I was told that I was a very sensitive boy, but this sensitivity didn't seem to affect me much because I had my share of fights at school.

I know I wasn't sensitive about being called names because we had a neighbours' boy and every time he called me a Nigger, and as he was of German extraction, I would call him a Hun. Other neighbours who lived not far from us were part-French and if these two ganged-up on me and my brothers we used to call them Huns and Froggies, so you see all in all, we had quite a happy childhood. Race relations never worried us. That was something that only came upon me after I had left school and after I had left home.

In the poem about the hunting trip, I first met this old chap who I wrote of, called Warru, when I went to Moore River Native Settlement when I had left school. This was a plan which my dad had to learn me and another brother who was about two years older than me to learn the rudiments of farming and to get us on to some land eventually. The few months I spent in Moore River Settlement was the first time I had met up with my own kind. Warru fascinated me. Although I was only fourteen years of age and he was a man of at least forty-five, he came from the North-west, the same area where my dad came from and he was of the same tribe. I used to spend many hours talking to him: he used to sing aboriginal songs and I used to write down the aboriginal words, and of course, the first chance I got to go hunting with him I was happy.

He was a remarkable man. He could track things which I couldn't see. He could also throw a spear forty or fifty feet, deadly accurate, and even a stone thrown at a bird, seven times out of ten he would bring the bird down. He had a beautiful voice and to hear him sing in his own language was something which I am afraid is lost because he has been dead for many years. His songs were something for Australian culture to remember.

The hunting trip him and I went on, we would go out and stay out all night, we would build a fire, pull down a few bushes for a wind-break and we might not even have a blanket. We'd have a bag in which we'd carry what we'd collected during the day and that bag would do us to lay on and with a fire each side of us we'd sleep quite warm and comfortable all night. He could walk for hours and hours and he didn't seem to look where he was going yet he'd finish up right on a soak or a waterhole, he'd know just exactly where it was. I'd be lagging behind by this time, you know, eight or nine mile, but he'd sit down and laugh, tell a few yarns, light a fire and cook a bit of meat, have a drink and away we'd go again.

Many years after, I met him in Perth. Of course I was twenty-eight years of age and he could only just remember me and half the time I think he just said he remembered me so that he could get a few bob off me. His eyesight had gone, he was dressed in hand-me-down clothing, he had taken to the drink—of course, he always chewed tobacco but now he smoked and I often saw him picking up butts in the street. He camped wherever he could, in parks, under bridges and that and one day I heard that they had found him dead in Wellington Square, curled around the butt of a tree. That was my friend Warru.

We'd hardly been back a month from Moore River Native Settlement, back home, when my father died. The farming venture had fallen through and Dad had decided that he wanted us boys home instead, there was better chances of employment at home. One of our greatest thrills was to go with the Old Man—us boys—of a Sunday morning and we would walk up into the hills and go hunting. Well, it was one of these days when my dad was killed with a bull. This paddock was a ring-barked paddock which we always cut through to go home—of course, on these Sunday hunting trips with the Old Man we'd walk fifteen to twenty miles—and it was getting late, just on dusk, and the farmer who owned this paddock had put a mob of cattle into it. We didn't know it then, but there was a Jersey bull in there and it chased us boys and my dad scooped up a handful of sticks and kept the cattle back until we'd got through the fence. Between the fence and where we last saw him standing, there was an irrigation ditch and as he leapt across it—although he was in his fifties, he could still run fast—and as he jumped the irrigation ditch, he tripped and hit his head on the opposite bank and it twisted his head around sharply and it broke his neck. That broke the family up properly and it was only eight weeks after that we left Yarloop. I've been back there a couple of times because I was always happy there, but Dad's death was the thing that really scattered our family.

My mother had always been an independent woman, strong, forceful character, would stand no interference from anyone.

One word from her was enough for us kids. When Dad was killed, she applied for help from the appropriate Authority and she was told that she would have to go to the then Aboriginal Department for assistance. You see, with Dad gone we were automatically thrown back under the care of the Aboriginal Department, but my mum was a proud woman. She refused all help from them—anyway, all the help she would have got would have been rations which consisted of tea, sugar, flour and soap which wasn't much good for a family of ten, so she went out to work for a living.

She took on washing, scrubbing, and although us older boys were able to clear out and look for work, she still had the six smaller ones at home to fend for which she did do until they grew up and got married. She assisted them in one way and another right up until the time of her death.

Life in the North-west was very different to life in Yarloop. But I loved the North. One time, as a matter of fact, I lived on an out-camp for two years on my own. I saw the Boss in that two years about eight or nine times. He came out periodically and I did go in for Christmas. Christmas Day is on the 25th of course, but having no calendar I went on the 26th, and of course most of the fun was over. But that was nothing. It was the country I liked.

This place where I was, was break-away country, the valley floor was down about three to four hundred feet; and the hills, which were sheer, were all around me. It was really beautiful country, stark, the green of spinifex; and when it did rain, which was seldom, the grass would green up very quickly, flowers would come out, live perhaps three or four days and then die. I used to feel that that particular piece of country was my own and there was many and many a piece of verse which I wrote and which I unfortunately lost or destroyed myself.

Don't forget, I wasn't always on my own. When I was on that out-camp, sometimes the tribes came through. At one time there was about four hundred and fifty camped there on their annual pingai—that's their walkabout—about seven miles from me and as I had a high-powered thirty-two and we had wild cattle on this station, I decided to shoot one and help them out with some meat. So I went down this particular day and shot a bull, scrub bull: he went about three miles before he dropped but I found him dead so then I let the air into his stomach so that he wouldn't blow up and I went back to the place where these people were all camped and told them where I had shot this bull and there was meat there if they wanted it.

I stayed with them that night and all next day until it got cool and then I went home. But I had really a wonderful time with these people. They broke up into little groups that night and one group started singing and I can still see the scene, the pool down the bottom of the hill with the gum-trees around it, their moving around in the moonlight, the windmill behind them where they could get water if they wanted it, although they had the creek, small fires dotted over the hill itself—a small hillside where they camped—you could hear them talking in their own language and now and then there'd be a burst of laughter.

This is the kind of scene I remember when I think of the full-blood aboriginal in the North. Mind you, they live a hard life by our standards, but then it's a hard country up there. These people have worked out a way of life of their own. They've proved it over hundreds of years. For instance, I can remember on one occasion on one station on which I worked in the North-west, an old aboriginal woman who would have been at least between the age of eighty or ninety years, although their ages are hard to tell. When she was a young lass of about sixteen, according to the usual tribal law, she had been given to a man much older than herself and she committed an unforgiveable sin—she ran away with a young man of another tribe. They were chased and they were caught and the young man was duly executed, speared to death, and the girl was held down on her stomach and fire-sticks were placed on her heel-tendons until they were shrivelled and she was effectively ham-strung. Of course, from the age of sixteen until she died at the age of ninety, this unfortunate soul had to crawl on her hands and knees for all her life. It was quite a common occurrence for me as I rode down past the aboriginal camp to visit a windmill which was about nine mile away, and I often crossed her tracks, or she crossed mine on the way back. I would see her tracks as she scuttled along on hands and knees to pick up firewood. Believe me, she was a pitiful sight, but tribal law is hard and these people do live with it.

One thing which struck me afterwards and which I was very concerned about was the loss of aboriginal culture, especially in Western Australia. Although there are some known aboriginal sacred grounds only sixty miles from Perth, only an hour and a half's drive, these have not been gazetted and I have found that many part-aboriginal youngsters, I would say up to the age of thirty, did not know how to make spears, boomerangs. This is a natural thing, I suppose. But one of the things which I was really alarmed at was the loss of the aboriginal language.

I had made attempts to learn this language many years before, not knowing it at the time, and I have managed to save at least half of it in my own memory; but then, over a period of three years, talking to different groups, visiting different people in different towns within an area of four hundred and fifty miles of Perth, I did find that it was possible to rediscover the language of the South-west tribes. Within the South-west tribes there were at least ten or twelve dialects spoken, but over all they were able to communicate through the language itself. These dialects were all of the Bibbulmum language.* The word "Bibbulmum" is two words —"bibbul", meaning "paper" and "mum" or "marm" meaning "father". These people were known as the "Paper-bark People". The reason for this was quite apparent as where the paper-bark tree grew there was water. The papery bark of these trees provided shelter for the building of mia-mias and gunyahs in times of rain, also there would be plenty of fish and bird-life and plenty of wild native vegetables. It took me about three years to save about two-thirds of the language, which I have done. According to the University, there are at

* See Appendix.

least a thousand words in each dialect which would be spoken or with which you would be able to carry on a conversation. I have managed to compile at least seven hundred and fifty words and this, I believe, is quite enough to carry on a conversation if one takes the trouble to learn the Bibbulmum language.

The happiest part of my life was definitely when I was a youngster. I think the best period was the 'thirties, or the late 'thirties, because nobody had anything. There was no work, there was lots of white people walking around with the seat out of their pants you might say. Aboriginal people didn't really worry because we had quite enough to eat, that is by present day standards, as I look back. We would stay out in the bush sometimes up to periods of three to four months. We caught kangaroos, we caught possums out of season, we sold the skins and occasionally, when we felt like it we would walk to town which was a distance of fourteen mile. But we usually stayed out on a farm, on the back blocks of the farm. We got a few days work from the farmer, because the farmer in those days had no money. They were really wonderful times when I look back because we had so much freedom, didn't have to worry about Social Service or anything like that because we did actually keep ourselves. All we had to have was flour, tea and sugar, a few spuds and onions. You could always get vegetables from somewhere and these were really happy times when I was from about the age of fifteen until about seventeen. That, I would say, was the happiest time of my life.

Contents

The First-born

Where are my first-born, said the brown land, sighing;
They came out of my womb long, long ago.
They were formed of my dust—why, why are they crying
And the light of their being barely aglow?

I strain my ears for the sound of their laughter.
Where are the laws and the legends I gave?
Tell me what happened, you whom I bore after.
Now only their spirits dwell in the caves.

You are silent, you cringe from replying.
A question is there, like a blow on the face.
The answer is there when I look at the dying,
At the death and neglect of my dark proud race.

Retrospect

When I was small
And oh, so tall
I looked for homes
Of elves and gnomes
Hiding in the clover.

I watched the sun's last gold array
Fade and fold the day away;
I heard the light's last laughing word
From the kookaburra bird;
I heard the wind and winter rains
On the high tin roof and the window panes.
There was little-boy bliss
In a mother's kiss,
Then the day was really over.

Man, don't yearn for the past to return,
The years have all passed over.
I know now there are many things
With hidden stings
Deep down in the clover.

The Boy and the Robin

The boy
Crouched behind a fallen tree,
Once a forest giant,
Arrow fitted to the home-made bow,
Taut but pliant.

The robin
No doubt had seen the boy before at play
Therefore
Had no fear of him throughout a day.

The robin fluffed himself against the cold
And sang.
The boy,
A hunter now, brave and bold,
Drew back the string and—twang!
The arrow sped but erred in flight
But broke the song.

The boy,
A killer now, flung the bow,
Forgetting right
From wrong
And with mingled joy and dread
Saw red feathers scatter from the blow
And the robin,
Broken, battered, lying dead.

The boy
Picked up the shattered bird
And strange emotions surged within his breast.
Crooning soothing, pitying words,
He smoothed the robin's vest.

A new sound now
Cut into the boy's despair,
For in the branches of a lower bough
A nest of tiny robins crying there.
And through the years that lay ahead,
To no man he admitted
The story of a robin, dead,
A crime a boy committed.

Camped in the Bush

Wind in the hair
Of a sleeping child
And the tree-tops wavering,
The starlight mild.

The moon's first peep
On the sand-plain rise,
And the fox in the shadows
With flashing eyes.

Over the campfire
The bat cries shrill
And a "semi" snarls
On the Ten Mile Hill.

And the lonely whistle
Of the train at night,
Where my kingdom melted
In the city's light.

The Children

The children walked through the bush together,
The girls apprehensive, wondering whether
This or that had stings:
Feminine, scared of crawling things.
    The boys playing tricks,
    Tickling them with black-boy sticks.
    One boy, brave with the ego of the male,
    Picked up a lizard by the tail,
Chased the tall blonde girl with the vacant stare.
She screamed, ran like a frightened hare,
But before he could reach her
She found the safety of the laughing teacher.
    Lunch time came, all food became the same
    For all upon the ground
    And made an appetizing mound
    Of cakes and pies and custard tarts.
The lizard-boy, not brave now, played his part
And placed beside the cake and ham
A thick stale slice of bread and jam.
Dumbly he sat, staring straight ahead,
    Embarrassed, wishing he were dead
    Or in some other place,
    The crimson rising in his face.
    Then suddenly he was aware
That there was someone there
Kneeling at his side,
The tall blonde girl, blue eyes wide,
Fair hair framing the oval face.
    And with a gentle grace that all could see
    She said softly: "Will you share your bread with me?"
    He looked at her and blinked away the tears.
    Suddenly the two of them were old beyond their years.
And in the bush surrounding green,
He was a prince and she was his queen.

The Boomerang

You cunningly contrived piece of wood—
According to my people you should
Return to me in a long, curving line:
That is your purpose and that's your design.

But for me this is not so,
Because I throw and throw.
My eyes are bleary,
I am arm-and-leg weary,
Right to the marrow.

Why, oh why didn't my ancestors
Invent the bow and arrow!

Death of a Snake

Six foot dugite of ebony sheen,
Gliding through granite where he can't be seen.

But the magpies shout "Look out!" And squawking:
"Boy, beware of where you're walking!"

He's moving faster, find a waddy!
Leaping breathless, crush that body.

Twisting, turning, belly yellow,
Now he's dead, a harmless fellow.

As meat to eat he's highly rated,
But alas, I'm too sophisticated.

Now find a place for him to rest,
So fling him on the bull-ants' nest.

Day Flight

I closed my eyes as I sat in the jet
And I asked the hostess if she would let
Me take on board a patch of sky
And a dash of the blue-green sea.

Far down below my country gleamed
In thin dry rivers and blue-white lakes
And most I longed for, there as I dreamed,
A square of the desert, stark and red,
To mould a pillow for a sleepy head
And a cloak to cover me.

Prejudice

Is this a game
      To you, white child,
This calling of a name?
      You ran away,
Fair hair flying,
      Blue eyes cruel and gay,
Leaving the dark child crying.
      Yesterday
She came home
      Sad, forlorn,
Puzzled by this sudden scorn.
      I watched her walk through the broken gate;
I thought,
      Is this destiny or fate,
Or God or man
      Who puts the value and the ban
On certain things
      Like skin and class,
And who will pass
      For what?
Who is to blame?
      All will rot.
Black and white decay the same.
      I could not tell her this:
I met her with a kiss
      And dried her tears,
Knowing that the years
      Will give her pride
And grace.
      She will not hide
But stand tall and proud,
      A member of her race.

Maureen

Eyes sparkling,
Teeth gleaming, a legacy of her race:
Hair soft and darkling
Framing the happy face.

Words stumbling and fumbling
In the search for the order of living.
Here is the young with a song to be sung
And a heart with the glory of giving.

But, child, there will be sorrow and pain
In the sun and the rain.
There will be moments of anger and doubt;
There will be cheating and lying
And paying with crying
As the whispering grows to a shout.

Wait, child.
There will also be love and laughter and caring,
Wonderful things which are made for the sharing—
The green of the earth, the countryside,
The blue of the sky, the whole world wide.
If you share your life with God and your kind
You will never be one who is left behind.

The Crippled Boy

If you could run, child,
I dream of you running wild,
Splashing through the creek,
Barefoot through the clover.
Everything you fancied you would seek
Before the day was over.
Patch would not have to walk with you
As now, side by side.
You would skim the earth,
Dog and boy,
Loving life for what it's worth,
Full of joy.
I see the gleaming brace beside your bed:
My mind like lace
And tightened thread,
Returns me from my fantasy, my son.
Yet, my loved one,
Have no fears.
You and I shall run:
I will hide my tears.
Our days will be spun
With golden mornings
Flecked with silver after rain.
Every day will be a wonder dawning
And I will hide the heartache and the pain, my son—
I will hide the heartache and the pain.

My Dog

You foolish creature charging in
To flop in my chair with your lop-sided grin,
You chew my shoes and eat my socks:
I'm sure your head is made of rocks.
I plant, you dig my flowers and lawn,
You bark when the roosters crow at dawn.
You chase the baker, you bit the rector,
But you seem to adore the bill-collector.
Chaos comes with you through the door—
You are a clown and not much more.

But when I sit by the fire at night
And the world is mostly sleeping,
My thoughts caught up in fancied flight,
Then gently you come creeping.

You sit and stare at me above you,
Your tongue-tip soft as a feather,
And I stretch my hand to prove I love you—
A man and his dog together.

The Spider Web

The web trembled, swayed,
Silver spun
And the light from the rising sun
Danced and played
On a thousand captured rain-drops from the dawn:
Winter lace displayed
Between the pear-tree and the rose-bush on the lawn.
The sun, now warm,
Set rain-drops free,
Beauty and form
Gone—naught left to see
As transient glories flow and ebb.
All that was left was a sticky, broken spider web.

Memory

Something once said
Cuts like a knife,
Scarring the memory of the dead.
Only regret is left, taunting
Through the years:
A face sad and haunting,
Wet with tears
Because of what was said.

The reply
Was quickly given, unthinking,
A cry,
A sob of pain
Robbed the hurt one of breath.
Because of the pride, unrelenting,
Only the bitter words remain
Accusing unto death.

The Painter

This is the canvas I can see:
Death in the park and misery;
The saddened face of a hungry child
With matted hair and eyes half wild;
An upraised hand, a blow on flesh,
The curious sound of tortured breath.

This scene so fills my mind and heart
I flex my fingers, turn to start;
But at the sound of one faint word
My colours run and all is blurred.

The Aboriginal Stockman

Hands gnarled, fingers calloused by the bridle-rein;
Hair white, hat well worn,
He prodded the sleepy fire.
And flame, tiny bright,
Lit the face
Lined with contours
Like the land which now eluded him.
Yet in return he loved and served
Despite what they had done.
The windmills, the miles of wire,
The endless riding—
And recompense?
A new check shirt, tobacco ...
But dreams, they were his alone.
He stirred the fire again
And pointed to the high hills.
That's where the food was,
My food, now long gone,
Not the Boss's bread and meat and tea.
He became silent,
The pipe between broken teeth;
His fingers plucked a coal
And broke the glow of embers,
And his features vanished in the sudden dark.
Quietly I rose and whispered gently,
"Good night, old man, good night."
A gesture small, and softer still the reply:
"Good night, my friend, good night."

The Black Tracker

He served mankind for many a year
Before the jeep or the wireless.
He walked, he loped, no thought of fear,
Keen-eyed, lithe and tireless.

He led Eyre to the western plains;
He went with Burke and Wills;
He put Nemarluk* back in chains:
He found the lost in the hills.

He found hair and spittle dry:
He found the child with relief.
He heard a mother's joyful cry
Or a mother's wail of grief.

He found the lost one crawling south,
Miles away from the track.
He siphoned water, mouth to mouth,
And carried him on his back.

He heard the white man call him names,
His own race scoffing, jeering.
"A black man playing white man games,"
They laughed and pointed, sneering.

No monument of stone for him
In your park or civilized garden.
His deeds unsung, fast growing dim—
It's time you begged his pardon.

* Nemarluk—Aboriginal murderer of the early 'nineties, captured after a long search by Bul-Bul, who is recognized as the greatest of Australia's black trackers.

Warru

Fast asleep on the wooden bench,
Arms bent under the weary head,
There in the dusk and the back-street stench
He lay with the look of the dead.

I looked at him, then back through the years,
Then knew what I had to remember—
A young man, straight as wattle spears,
And a kangaroo hunt in September.

We caught the scent of the 'roos on the rise
Where the gums grew on the Moore;
They leaped away in loud surprise,
But Warru was fast and as sure.

He threw me the fire-stick, oh what a thrill!
With a leap he sprang to a run.
He met the doe on the top of the hill,
And he looked like a king in the sun.

The wattle spear flashed in the evening light,
The kangaroo fell at his feet.
How I danced and I yelled with all my might
As I thought of the warm red meat.

We camped that night on a bed of reeds
With a million stars a-gleaming.
He told me tales of Noong-ah* deeds
When the world first woke from dreaming.

He sang me a song, I clapped my hands,
He fashioned a needle of bone.
He drew designs in the river sands,
He sharpened his spear on a stone.

*Noong-ah—Aboriginal tribe of the south-west of Western Australia.

I will let you dream—dream on, old friend—
Of a boy and a man in September,
Of hills and stars and the river's bend—
Alas, that is all to remember.

Yadabooka*

The desert wind, the harsh sun, your tribal land
Is part of you, your very soul.
How can a stranger understand?
Better the retribution of angry spears
Than the slow sure death of prison years.
They will talk of you over shining table tops
And cups of tea.
They will write of you in legal terms,
Make plans to set you free.
But this desert black, this Stone Age man,
Must be made to understand
And with a power like God they brand
A thousand years into the pattern of today.
They will soon forget you, Yadabooka,
The very same who built the frame
To mould these laws
Do not remember Namatjira.
Cry, cry in your new world of stone, desert dweller!
Cry for distant places in the sun.
All this will have answer in a morning
When ignorance is answered
And the final race is run.

* Yadabooka—a tribal relative of the author's father who is still serving
a life sentence for a ritual killing in the Port Hedland district.

*Laverton Incident**

The two worlds collided
In anger and fear
As it has always been—
Gun against spear.

Aboriginal earth,
Hungry and dry,
Took back the life again,
Wondering why.

Echo the gun-blast
Throughout the land
Before more blood seeps
Into the sand.

* Laverton is 470 miles from Perth, W.A., in the eastern goldfields area. In September 1969 an aboriginal named Raymond Watson was wounded in the leg by a police officer during a disturbance, and subsequently died in hospital. The case caused controversy in Aboriginal circles throughout Australia.

The Artist

He squats on a narrow ledge in the summer shade;
A spear and an axe of stone lay at his side:
The wilgy,* gently moulded, mixed with care and pride,
For which, in the last time of rain,
He walked a hundred miles to trade.

He thought of his totem brother,
The eagle-hawk, and smiled.
Yet he could not trace his brother on the stone
For they were flesh and feather, bone of bone,
And this was the law and not to be defiled.

Time goes by, he sits back satisfied,
His work alone,
The emu in full flight,
Stark and clear, outlined in wilgy white
Against the black and brown and reddened weatherbeaten
    stone.

There's a gleaming handrail around the ledge today.
The hawk whistles vainly for his vanished brother.
He glares at blue-rinsed tourists clicking camera at each other
And skitters aloft, an angry flight,
From the parlour-coach, all gleaming bright,
On the bitumen road a hundred yards away.

---

* Wilgy—the paint or ochre (red, white or blue) used by Aborigines in corroborees and initiation ceremonies.

Dingo Dingo

She ran, swift and low, at the close of the day,
Testing the wind, her head held high.
The far-away plain was her nightly run,
And back in the cave the young pups whined.

She moved like a wraith through the desert gums,
Skirting the creek where tracks would show,
Threading her way through rock-strewn ground,
The miles passed under her running stride.

The man lay flat at the foot of the cave,
The rifle held in his slender hands,
Stealth and patience were part of him,
Hat pulled low to shutter the moon.

She came through the gap at the edge of the plain,
Looked at the sheep with hungry eyes:
Sank on her belly, creeping up close,
Pointing her ears at the sleeping prey.

The moonlight captured the scene of death.
She sprang at the throat of the nearest lamb.
The old ewe turned, too late, too late,
And met the same fate as her dying young.

The dingo gorged on the flesh of the kill,
Picked up the lamb in her trap-like jaws
And began her run to the distant cave
With the food she'd won for her hungry ones.

A blood-red dawn had painted the east
When at last she reached the edge of the range.
She paused and tested the air about her
Then soft and clear she called to her young.

In an instant, frozen, she saw the Man
Between herself and the secret cave;
She dropped the lamb as the bullet struck,
Her yellow coat ran crimson then.

The rising sun caught the scene of death.
The hunter deftly handled the kill:
He thought of what he could buy his young
And with a smile he turned for home.

Skeletal

You are a point of interest,
Old bones in a museum case.
A card reads: THIS IS A SKELETON OF A
MEMBER OF THE ABORIGINAL RACE.

I wonder where you laid your head at night
When you roamed the banks of the Swan.
Perhaps you walked to Karla-munda
And on, and on,
By the marsh, by the reeds,
And gathered there your Jam and Wattle seeds.

You swam with reeds upon your head
And pulled the sleeping duck down under.
You knew the feel of rain on your face,
Lightning flash, the crack of thunder.

Yes, Old One, you knew how to live.
You had no need of white man's legislation.
What you could see was yours, supreme,
The earth and sky out of a dream
Was your Creation.

Fancy is gone, my dream of you is broken
By children rushing in the dim-lit room.
I touch the show-case gently as a token
And I hear him whisper: "Courage",
Through the darkness and the gloom.

The Accident

Fair, fair is the world of the young today
With a love of life and heart so gay.
The other two will be here at eight,
Then away to the fun of a Saturday date.

Boy's gleaming car is polished, neat.
The four of them will have a treat.
One happy child in a new coat, gay,
And a fresh hair-do in the modern way.
Her name is Teen, without a care,
Her skirt is fab, her feet are bare.

Quick, boy: there's a car on the curve ahead.
Pass before the lights turn red!
A screech of rubber, spinning wheels,
A crash of glass, a scream congeals
As a windscreen slashes a pretty throat.
There's a change of colour on the duffle coat.

Doll-like bodies on the bitumen freeze,
Young eyes, vacant, stare at death.
A boy moans, "Help me, help me, please",
In a shuddering gasping fight for breath.

The ambulance wails, a requiem giving:
The lights blink green, then red.
The attendants curse and look for the living:
No need to worry the dead.

My Brother, My Sister

There's a gleam of the moon on the man on the rim-rock:
His arm, lifted high, flashes down in an arc.
The kangaroo runs, spins, leaping and tumbling
And falls to the ground with a spear through the heart.

When they hunt in the swamp it's a piccannin morning,
Then the water-hen ripples away from her nest.
Oh, this harvest of food is truly God-given
For life has a purpose and love's at its best.

Then the sheep and the cattle came over the ranges:
They flattened the grasses and muddied the waters.
The uron* and carda crawled into the boulders
And the bigorda is hiding behind the full moon.

Come, brother, come into the townships and cities.
There's food and there's drink, all yours for the asking,
A house, near-condemned, some clothing to match it
And a Guv'ment man with his tongue in his cheek.

Come Marpoo, bring Jeeri: she's young and becoming.
She's frightened, we know, but we show her the way.
We show her the brute and the beast that is in us,
Then turn her loose in the city to play.

Oh, my people, my people! You are the changelings.
The neon lights flicker: "Kia-ora Saloon".
The kangaroo comes from the shop on the corner.
My brother, my sister, you are dying too soon.

---

* Uron—the bob-tailed goanna. Carda—the race-horse goanna. Bigorda—
the hill-kangaroo.

Lost

I have seen the plant grow,
Seed burst and the blanket of earth
Slip back to show
The white-green stem of new birth.

I have seen ring-bark strangle the Wandoo:
Grey arms and fingers, a silhouette high
As if she begged a rendezvous
With dead friends in the sky.

I have watched the changing weather
Scatter clouds as if at play;
Caught the drifting emu feather
And wore it in my hair throughout the day.

I have watched a thin moon rinse a valley in its new light;
Stepped wary, ready to apply
A stick to back of tiger-snake or dugite:
Poked my tongue at lizard in reply.

All I hear now are machine-made sounds.
Lost is the life that quickened me.
Telephone, paper-clip, convention abounds.
Your civilization has sickened me!

Slum Dwelling

Big brown eyes, little dark Australian boy
Playing with a broken toy.
This environment his alone,
This is where a seed is sown.
Can this child at the age of three
Rise above this poverty?

The walls all cracked and faded, bare.
The glassless windows stare and stare
Like the half-dead eyes of a dying race . . .
A sad but strange, compelling place.

Whither?

So they said: "Go to school."
This was the rule.
This was the yard-stick of advancement in a society
Which, with clasped hands and piety,
Spoke of equality within the eyes of God and the law.
Yet somewhere there was a flaw,
Because they told one man, "Don't spit on the street", but he
    spat;
To the other, "Off the street at six", and that was that.
No time to weep or wail.
If we protested, by six-thirty we were behind the walls of a
    country jail.
So we stayed on the Reserve in isolated peace.
Now and again we saw the police
Take the brown-skinned child,
Tearful, subdued, half wild.
Then the disciples came in deep contrition:
"Mother, father, they're better off upon a Mission.
We will lead them out of blindness,
Smother them with loving kindness."
Yet, at fourteen we were too old to keep,
So they said, "Go, brother, and what ye sow, ye shall reap."
To show them we would adopt their kind of sense
We would stay on the high white side of the fence. . . .
"Have they come to live in our street?"
Stung to reply, we said, "These are your footsteps made by
    your feet.
We must follow the trousered leg and the leather shoe.
To be what you want, we must imitate you."
So the two societies met and some fell apart.
This then was the start
For a search for a patch of blue. The park
Became our home in the after-dark.
We sat with arms around our knees;

Some of us curled up and died around the boles of trans-
    planted trees:
We crept under bridges looking for vacant ground.
Here we were safe from the sound of the city street
And the Rat-van on its nightly beat,
And the empty bottles shrieked a sign
Of a stupefied brain and red, red wine;
Of lemonade laced for little "white-ladies".
Is that our making our own kind of Hades?
So leave us now to continue our crying,
There's nothing left for us now but the terror of dying.

*Family**

We would like to visit our brother today.
We're new here, fresh from a country town.
We would like to talk of folks far away
And the life we led as children.

How we gathered the tails at lambing time:
They sizzled and curled on the open fire.
We followed the plough at seeding time
And screamed at the plovers, wheeling.

We teased the bull at the edge of the dam,
Mocking his rumbling and roaring.
Squinting our eyes at the glare of the sun,
How we envied the brown hawk soaring.

We circled the rabbit, crouching low,
And he fled from our do'aks† flying,
Darting, dodging too quickly for Brindle
Who yelped with the effort of trying.

Shearing time was a time of fun
Cadging the cakes at Smoke-oh time,
Culling the best of the sheep each run
For Joe who was after his hundred.

This is the pattern your ordered mind
Has forgotten, this way of perceiving
That survival through sharing and sharing, my friend,
Was a Carpenter's way of believing.

* This poem was inspired by the sentencing of two aborigines to three
months jail for leaving a country Reserve without permission, to visit a
brother in the Allawah Grove housing settlement.
  † Do'aks—throwing-sticks.

Aboriginal Reserve

The long low sweeping ground,
The horizon black in starlight
And somewhere now the sound
Of a child's cry in the night.

They stir a fire that is dying,
The sparks fly upward blending
With night and a people crying.
O where, O where is the ending?

The mind forgets tomorrow,
Eyes grow dull with the years,
Afraid of the heights of sorrow
And to fathom the depths of fears.

The Drifters

We are the drifters, the faceless ones.
Turn your heads as we walk by.
We are the lost, forgotten sons,
Bereft in a land of plenty.

Where is the spear of the days gone by?
No more the chant of the hunting song:
The laughing face and the laughing eyes,
So sad in a land of plenty.

We have lost the peal of the Mission bell,
Drowned out by the sounds of the city streets.
We have lots to say and none to tell
Of hell in a land of plenty.

Oh, this earth! This sun! This sky I see
Is part of my heart, my heritage!
Oh God, I cry. Cry God for me,
For a place in a land of plenty.

Desolation

You have turned our land into a desolate place.
We stumble along with a half-white mind.
Where are we?
What are we?
Not a recognized race . . .
There is desert ahead and desert behind.

The tribes are all gone,
The boundaries are broken:
Once we had bread here,
You gave us stone.

We are tired of the benches, our beds in the park,
We welcome the sundown that heralds the dark.
White Lady Methylate!
Keep us warm and from crying.
Hold back the hate
And hasten the dying.

The tribes are all gone,
The spears are all broken:
Once we had bread here,
You gave us stone.

A Nightmare of Reality

I stood alone on the top of the world
With hope and truth like a flag unfurled.

Under my feet was a blood-red haze
And the scream and the din of the pop-group craze.

A handsome boy, like a beardless goat,
Pranced and danced in a shimmering coat;

A beautiful girl, her hair dyed pink,
Giggled past with a black-eyed wink.

A million men in a million shrouds
Sat and talked on thunder clouds.

"Wars, disease and the common cold
Put them all in the same dark mould."

So I kicked the world round the opposite way
And even God had nothing to say.

The Red Gum and I

Kudden, huge and tall,
You still belong.
Take me through the bark
Into the sap stream.

Wash away this dirty white
That clings and smells
Of platitudes and Hells to me.
Take me through the wood, your heart,
High, to the leaves, cool green leaves
That reach for the sky.
Press them to my eyes, my ears,
So I can shut out glib tongues,
Fears and promises like worms
That twist and churn within my mind,
Enter my brain, then out again.

Help us, kudden,
Take us back where we belong.

A Eulogy for Peace—
by an Old Aboriginal

Why don't white man sit down quiet by fire?
   Not stand up and call other country-fella liar.
What white-fella want to talk about fight for?
   Everybody have plenty, still want more.
He have big house,
   Money in pocket,
Yet he not satisfied:
   Want to make bigger rocket.
One day, I bet, pretty damn soon
   Rocket go straight like spear,
Put man on moon.
   Then, I bet, plenty trouble,
Moon and earth burst like bubble.
   People go round like leaf in willy-willy,
Tear their hair,
   All sorry and silly.
White-fella and him piccannin die in city,
   Black-fella in bush, he feel pity.
White-fella wrong, call each other liar,
   Should have sat down quiet and talked by fire.

Integration

Let these two worlds combine,
Yours and mine.
The door between us is not locked,
Just ajar.
There is no need for the mocking
Or the mocked to stand afar
With wounded pride
Or angry mind,
Or to build a wall to crouch and hide,
To cry or sneer behind.

This is ours together,
This nation—
No need for separation.
It is time to learn.
Let us forget the hurt,
Join hands and reach
With hearts that yearn.

Your world and mine
Is small.
The past is done.
Let us stand together,
Wide and tall
And God will smile upon us each
And all
And everyone.

Appendix

A BIBBULMUM VOCABULARY

(Compiled by the author for the Western Australian Aboriginal Association)

ah woon	a jocular expression
allawah	look out
allee	there
alleja	over there
arn	over
baalapiny	theirs
baal-nicha warrah mut	this person is no good
baal un	he did
baalup	his or hers
balga	blackboy
banban	butterfly
bardee	succulent grub
bardupup	rushes
barkanyiny	biting
barminy	strike
bar warngeiny	talking wrongly
beark	pig
bearn	strangle
bearung	prickle
beely	navel
beeringiny	sniff the wind
beerniny	choking
beerr	fingernail
beert	sinew
beeruk	summer
berri	fingernails
bibbul	paper
bibbulbu	paperbark-tree
billbarl	black long-tail goanna (never eaten)
birrndi	girl when she reaches the age of puberty
bitjarr	sleep
bitjarra	sleeping

bo	afar; a long way off
bok	clothing
bonich	knee
boogaja	going to a particular place
boojarra	ground
boolya	magical powers
boolya-duk	one with magical powers
boorlba	rifle
boorlgoo	narcotic mixed with ashes
boorn	stick
boorna-karla	firestick
boorndi	large rock or stone
boy	stone
boya	money
boyaginy	a huge area of rock
bridarra	important person
bujep	bushes
bukely	hit; strike; slap
bungarra	lizard
bunja	old man
burnunginy	this way or that way
carda	race-horse goanna
cart	head
cart darabiny	thinking
carti	hills
ceech	small spear
cheak	wild fruit
choo choo	shame
chook	sister
chookiny	sister-in-law
churditch	native cat
colbirri	wild berry
conk	uncle
coomal	possum
coong	rib
coonga	the side
coorawoorong	disbelief
coorlung	child
coorlunga	children
coort	heart
coyche	axe
daarwet	York gum
dar	mouth

dara-but	dumb
darlyinniny	go swiftly at a run
darp	knife
darwarrah	virulent tongue
dillabert	plover
dillert	type of lizard
dirdong	springtime
dirl-dirl	bellbird
diyll	spit
diyllinniny	spitting
do'ak	throwing-stick
doniny	the act of doing something
dookaniny	close to
dorrl	knock
dorrliny	knocking
dubakiny	slowly
dubakiny-koorl	go slowly
dubakiny-koorliny	going slowly
dugatch	snake
dulong	tongue
dumarlark	parrot
dwankabut	deaf
dwirt	dog
dwirtuck	dogs
dytch	meat
gnannory	eating
gnarn	eat
gnayl	arm-pit
gwinnen	duck
jaduluk-maradong	night
janark	evil spirit
jarraly	jarrah-tree
jeerp	grass
jeerung	fat
jen	foot
jendal	grey
jenna	both feet
jenna-amarra jenna-amarra	method of counting (5x5x5)
jenna-jen	footmark
jennt	eyebrows
jerdaluk	grey one
jerri	four

jittong	small lizard
jitty-jitty	willy wagtail
joiny	hair
joorp	kidney
joort	wart
jopuly	splash
juerl	bone
juerlarra	bony; thin
jurrnt	stars
ka	smile
kaen	one
ka-ka	laugh
ka-ka winniny	laughing
kant	camp
karl	hot coals
karla	fire; large fire
karla-munda	place of big fires
karla-murruny	act of burning
karlawooliny	hot
karl-dookanini	sit close to the fire
karl-teerdup	ashes
karrluk	home
karrung	anger; angry
kart	head
kartabooka	headwear
kart warrah	mad
keape	water
keearl	smoke
keert	run
keertarniny	walking swiftly
keertkoorliny	running
kia	yes
kinya	shame
kippilly	wet
kippillyuny	sopping wet
kobble	stomach
kobble a coort	the fat one
kobble a juerlarra	the thin one
kobble weert	hungry
kooant	camp near water
koobeeaku	owl
koojal	two
kookanjerrie	sheep
koolbardie	magpie

koolya	mud
koolya mut	telling lies
koolyawa	teller of lies
koolyung	wattle-tree
koomba	large
koong	rib
koonga	side
koonga-mia	house on the side of a hill
koongart	carry on shoulder
koonyell	turkey
koony uk	west
koorawarong	pleasant disbelief
koorliny	going some place
koornden	clouds (storm clouds)
koorndie	stone
koorndilla	thunder
koornt	water
kooyl	lice
kugardu	north
kurnaminy	when man and woman meet
kurnarn	true
kurnarnjul	is that true?
kurnarnkoorliny	truly going
kurnn	truth
kurrden	redgum-tree
kurrum	anyhow
kutich	think; understand
kuttajinoong	see and understand
kuttah	make believe
kuttaminy	going quickly
kuttiny	small lizard
kwan	posterior
kwark	skin hanging; kangaroo skin
kwear	frog
kwelly	sheoak-tree
kwirr	brush kangaroo
kwirnading	home of the brush kangaroo
kwobbinyarn	excellent
kwoliny	wrist
kwont	carpet snake (edible)
kwooinyga	very small
kylie	boomerang
marjen marjen	method of counting (5+5+5+5)
marlee	swan

marluck	thicket
marlup	unknowing
marm	father
marn-jarraly	burnt trees
marnk	tea
marp	skin
marr	hand; five
marri	wind
marri warabiny	rolling, billowing of cloud
marroo	sky
marruk donwarriny	gesture; wave of the hand
marudony	night
marwit	baby son
meak	moon
mear	lip
meear	liver
meeowl	eyes
meerl	ankle
meernapiny	jealous
meeroo	spear-thrower
meowlbirt	blind
merriny	flour
merrinyuk	bread (raw state)
mia	camp; wurlie
miar	green leaves
midjaul	rain
milly milly	paper
mimben	eyebrow
mimmy	female breast
minabru	dance; corroboree
mindalong	sandplain bush
mindich	sick
minga	ant
mirdarr	dance; corroboree
mirreeup	hurry
mo	three
mobyrne	magic
monaych	police officer
moodgar	Christmas-tree
mooly	nose
moonie	black
moonnawooliny	black night; blackness
moora wa	which hand
moorditch	good
moorga	winter

moorick	death by magic
moorick barm	strike with magic
moorlin	back
moych	swamp country
moylyup	sulking
moyup	snake
mugarlgurruk	sandplain-tree
mulgar	thunder, lightning or storm
mullarp	not knowing
mumbagee	where the river and sea meet
mumboyet	sea
mundik	prickle-bush
mungart	jam-tree
munjarly	damper
munjong	old fellow
murndong	silly genial fellow
mut	particular person or object
muttilly	dirty
narch cuttijarn	what are you thinking about?
narch wanginy	what do you mean by talking?
narri-giny	plenty of bluegums
narrnuk	back of neck
neerluk	carry under the arm
neernt	tail
neerwariny	sandflies
ngank	sun
ngank burlunginy	sunrise
ngank weerdiny	sunset
ngannuk	whiskers
ngarnk	mother
ngeean	who
ngertiny	cold
ngiy	cry (n.)
ngiyiny	crying
ngiy ngiyiny	crying continuously
ngook	honey
ngoolya	brother-in-law
ngoon	brother
ngoonyung	sweet
ngoopo	blood
ngoopulyuny	bleeding
ngoorndiny	to lie down
ngoort	horse
ngorluk	teeth

ngoyung	elbow
ngumbally	greedy fellow
ngummaree	tobacco
ngunoor	full beard
ngunung	mine only
nguny	mine
ngurll	me
ngurluk	mine (emphatically)
ngurrity	ribs
ngut	true
ngwirr	bandicoot; ring-tail possum
ni	see
niny	this
noobaritch	little child
noongar	Aboriginal of the Bibbulmum and south-
ern tribes	
noonuk	you
noonukiny	you did
noorak	egg
noort	flies
nop	boy
noych	dead
noycha	dying
noycha ngoorndiny	lying dead
nullong	that article or particular thing
nyarnyee	young of the kangaroo or any animal—
	bird or fish or reptile
nyearn wooning	disbelief
nyett	a little
nygar	what
nyindy	itchy
nyingarn	echidna
nyoondeak	brains
nyorn	pity
nyornditch	pitiful person
pin	plenty
waardiny	looking for some particular thing
waddy	club
wadjallah	white man
wadjullung	two or more white men
wagerup	plenty of emus
waitch	emu
waitch-in	emus

48

waitch-up	place of the emu
wal-waliny	crying, tears
wangeiny	talking
wank	talk
wannaniny	sneak along so no one can see you
wappalyung	big
wareluk	joint
warlitch	hawk
warna	digging and fighting stick used by women
warnboo	rug of kangaroo skin
warrah	bad
warrah-na	bad place
warrdiny	doing
warrdong	crow
warrnt	white gum
wayarniny	frightened
wearlany	unaware of
weerallo	expression of woe
weerlo	curlew
weerluk	salmon gum
weern	weak
weert	hungry
wilbra	rabbit
wilgy	paint used in corroborees
willy	flight of the kylie
willyuwa	wattle
winjar	where
winjar koorliny	where are you going?
winy	whistle
winyarn	poor fellow
winyinniny	whistling
wiyll-wiyll	swinging
woja woorliny	naked
woolah	shout of praise for an achievement
woonana	like this; in this fashion
woonarna	back to back
woonert	mallet-tree
wooniny	a word conveying disbelief
woort	away
woort koorl	go away
woort koorliny	going away
wopulyung	huge
wort	throat
wort beerniny	choking
wubbert	skull

yandi	a carrying utensil
yanjet	bulrushes
yarch	night owl
yarginy	turtle
yatch	bone
yet	jaw
yidarr	up
yidarra	in the act of going upward
yimmung	forehead
yimniny	here and there
yok	woman
yoki	shout of victory
yonga	kangaroo
yonga-up	plenty of kangaroos
yongurra	more than one kangaroo
yuart	nothing; no
yubaroo	south

WORDS DERIVED FROM ENGLISH

boordin	pudding
burleak	bullock
car-ich	motor car
Gubmin	the Government
ngoop	wine

PLACE NAMES OF THE BIBBULMUM

Balga	balga—the blackboy
Gin Gin	jenna-jen—footmark
Kalamunda	karla-munda—place of big fires
Katanning	keentarniny—walking swiftly
Konongorring	kurnarnkoorliny—truly going

Koongamia	koonga-mia—house on the side of a hill
Mandurah	marn-jarraly—burnt trees
Marradong	marudony—night
Mingenew	mingana—*from* minga, the ant
Morawa	moora wa—which hand
Narrogin	narri-giny—plenty of bluegums
Ongerup	yonga-up—plenty of kangaroos
Pingelly	pin-juerli—bones a-plenty
Pinjarra	pin-jarraly—plenty of trees
Quairading	kwirnading—home of the brush kangaroo
Wagerup	waitch-up—place of the emu
Wagin	waitch-in—emus
Wanneroo	*from* warna—the women's fighting and digging stick
Waroona	warrah-na—a bad place